The Read and Learn Series

Read 100

100-Word Reading Passages
for
Fact, Fiction, and Fun
at the
800-Word Level

Andrew E. Bennett

PRO LINGUA  ASSOCIATES

Pro Lingua Associates, Publishers

P.O. Box 1348, Brattleboro, Vermont 05302 USA
Office: 802 257 7779 • Orders: 800 366 4775
Email: info@ProLinguaAssociates.com
WebStore: www.ProLinguaAssociates.com
SAN: 216-0579

*At Pro Lingua
our objective is to foster an approach
to learning and teaching that we call
interplay, the interaction of language
learners and teachers with their materials,
with the language and culture,
and with each other in active, creative,
and productive play.*

Copyright © 2006 by Andrew E. Bennett
Adapted from an original Taiwanese edition, copyright © 2004 by Andrew E. Bennett

All rights reserved. No part of this publication may be reproduced or transmitted in any form or by any means, electronic, mechanical, photocopying, recording, or other, or stored in any information storage or retrieval system without permission in writing from the publisher.

ISBN 0-86647-232-0

This book was written and designed by Andrew E. Bennett. The Read & Learn edition was adapted for Pro Lingua by Raymond C. Clark. The design was adjusted by Arthur A. Burrows. It was printed and bound by Worzalla in Stevens Point, Wisconsin.

Cover by James Borstein, Corporate Communications: Design

Image Credits:

    Gui Yu: p. 2 (© Andrew E. Bennett)
    EnA: pp. 16, 22 (bottom), 30, 38, 42 (top) (© EnA Digital Arts)
    Hemera/Big Box of Art: pp. 4, 8, 16, 22 (top, second from top, third from top), 26, 30, 48, 54, 62, 64 (bottom right), 66, 70, 78 (© Hemera)
    Art Explosion 750,000: pp. 10 (© Nova Development)
    Corel: pp. 6, 20, 28, 32, 42 (bottom), 46, 60, 64 (top left, top right, bottom left), 74, 80 (© Corel)
    iStockPhoto: pp. 52 (© iStock Photo)
    A-Tai: pp.12, 44 (© Andrew E. Bennett)
    Paintings of Williams sisters © AA Burrows based on anonymous news photos
    Idea Design Center: p.26 (left), 36 (© Idea Design Center)
    DnJ: p. 26 (right) (©Dance & Jump Software)
    Mixa: pp. 34 (© Dainippon Screen Mfg Co.)
    Andrew E. Bennett: pp. 40, 58 (© Andrew E. Bennett)
    Idea Design Graphics: pp. 50, 72 (© Idea Design Graphics)
    Werner Forman Archive: p.68 (© Werner Forman Archive)
    Q Vision: p. 76 (© Q Vision)

Printed in the United States of America.
First edition. First Printing 2006. 2,000 copies in print.

Contents

	Welcome	1
Unit 1	On-Line Computer Games	2
Unit 2	My Best Friend	4
Unit 3	River Taxis	6
Unit 4	Weather Reports	8
Unit 5	Trans-Canada Railroad	10
Unit 6	Cold Soup	12
Unit 7	Venus and Serena Williams	14
Unit 8	The Last Day of the Last Class	16
Unit 9	Email: Summer Plans	18
Unit 10	Castles	20
Unit 11	Express Your Opinions	22
Unit 12	Credit Card Receipt	24
Unit 13	Journal	26
Unit 14	Superstitions	28
Unit 15	Disagreeing	30
Unit 16	Kyoto	32
Unit 17	Music Sales	34
Unit 18	Elephants	36
Unit 19	The Card Game	38
Unit 20	9 Ball	40

Contents

Unit 21	Flower Gardening	42
Unit 22	Seeing a Doctor	44
Unit 23	Personal Website	46
Unit 24	Old Friends	48
Unit 25	Tai Shan	50
Unit 26	Magazine Cover	52
Unit 27	Habits	54
Unit 28	Instant Message	56
Unit 29	Profile of an English Teacher	58
Unit 30	Music of Korea: The Changgo	60
Unit 31	Modern Heroes	62
Unit 32	Making a Cheese Sandwich	64
Unit 33	Summer Music Festival	66
Unit 34	Great Zimbabwe	68
Unit 35	Asking for Advice	70
Unit 36	Falling Rain	72
Unit 37	Persian Rugs	74
Unit 38	Safe Driving	76
Unit 39	Sign Language	78
Unit 40	Global Positioning System	80
	Answer Key	82
	For the Teacher	90

Welcome

Dear Reader,

   Welcome to Book Three in the Read and Learn Series. You can read about the world we live in -- our home and the places in it. You can read about the things we do -- work, play, travel, study, shop, talk, email, and eat. And you can learn a lot of useful English.

   There are 40 units in this book. Each unit has a reading and three exercises. The units are easy to do.

- Do the reading
- Do the exercises
- Check your answers (the answers start on page 82)

But first, you should understand these instructions before you begin to work.

>   ____ Write the correct word in each blank.
>
>   ____ Fill in the blank with the best answer.
>
>   ____ Put the words in the correct order.
>
>   ____ Complete each sentence.
>
>   ____ Match each question with the correct answer.
>
>   ____ Match each sentence with a response.
>
>   ____ Combine the two sentences into one sentence.

Now, read and learn and enjoy the book.

Pro Lingua Associates

1 On-Line Computer Games

Before the Internet, people usually played computer games at home, either alone or with a few friends. The Internet is now fast and cheap, and computer gaming is changing. With a computer connected to the Internet, people around the world can play their favorite games together.

There are many kinds of on-line computer games. Some are for playing sports, chess, and other traditional games. Others are "role playing" games. In these games, each player becomes a character in an on-line world. On-line computer gaming is a fast-growing business with a very exciting future. And it's a lot of fun!

Vocabulary

Choose the best answer.

1. Everything in today's cities _____ so quickly!
   A: becomes   B: changes   C: plays   D: is

2. The _____ is very big, but it's easy to fly to other countries.
   A: future   B: business   C: sport   D: world

3. I don't like to be _____. I prefer to be with friends.
   A: alone   B: fun   C: fast   D: together

4. Do you like _____ music or modern pop music?
   A: cheap   B: favorite   C: traditional   D: fast-growing

Reading

Choose the best answer.

1. (   ) To play on-line computer games, people need _____.
   A: a very expensive computer
   B: a fast-growing business
   C: a lot of friends at home
   D: a computer and an Internet connection

2. (   ) According to the reading, the Internet is _____.
   A: very expensive
   B: not fast enough for on-line computer games
   C: cheap, but slow
   D: changing the way people play computer games

3. (   ) What kind of computer game is **not** discussed?
   A: Role playing games.   B: Strategy games.
   C: Traditional games.   D: Sports games.

4. (   ) Which of the following is true?
   A: Every computer is connected to the Internet.
   B: The earliest computers could play games on-line.
   C: There is more than one kind of on-line computer game.
   D: In on-line chess games, people become characters.

Grammar

Write the correct past tense form in each blank.

1. We _____ games all last weekend.
   (played/play)

2. I _____ emails to a few friends yesterday.
   (send/sent)

3. Tina _____ her internet address yesterday.
   (changed/change)

4. Yesterday's game _____ so much fun!
   (were/was)

2 My Best Friend

Vera was my best friend. We met several years ago in elementary school. Vera was average height, with long dark hair. She had large dark eyes.

Singing and reading were two of her hobbies. She also liked swimming in her free time.

Vera was very smart and funny. I always laughed at her jokes. She had a really good personality, and everyone liked being with her. Vera was usually in a good mood, but sometimes she got sad. Then I listened to her and offered advice. We were always there for each other, in good times and bad. Since she moved away, I haven't heard from her, but I remember.

Vocabulary

Write the correct word in each blank.

| personality | height | mood | advice | hobby |

1. Rainy weather puts me in a bad _____.

2. I want to buy a new car. Can you give me some _____?

3. My _____ is building model ships. I love the sea.

4. Tom has a great _____. He's very easy to get along with.

Reading

Choose the best answer.

1. (　) Vera and the writer _____.
   - A: don't know each other very well
   - B: became friends recently
   - C: went to the same elementary school
   - D: are always in the same class together

2. (　) Vera _____.
   - A: has short hair
   - B: likes to tell jokes
   - C: has few friends
   - D: is often sad

3. (　) Which of the following is **not** one of Vera's hobbies?
   - A: Writing.
   - B: Swimming.
   - C: Singing.
   - D: Reading.

4. (　) Vera says, "I have a big problem." How might the writer respond?
   - A: "That's not my problem."
   - B: "Tell me about it. Maybe I can help."
   - C: "You should ask someone else for advice."
   - D: "It's your fault."

Grammar

Put the words in the correct order.

1. Saturday   usually   We   go   on   swimming

   _____.

2. sometimes   is   She   funny   very

   _____.

3. listen   to   ready   always   she   Is

   _____?

3 River Taxis

In Thailand, a country full of rivers, river taxis can be a good way to get around. These boats act much like buses on city streets. People can wait at a boat stop, on the riverside. The boats stop to let people on and off.

In some of Thailand's cities, like Bangkok, street traffic can be very bad. Using a river taxi can save a lot of time. For example, many boats go up and down the Chao Phraya River in Bangkok. Many of Bangkok's interesting sights are near the river. So taking a boat can be a great way for visitors to see that part of the city.

Vocabulary

Choose the best answer.

1. The _____ in the city gets really bad at 5:00 p.m.
   A: boat   B: traffic   C: taxi   D: street

2. The heavy rain made the _____ rise very high.
   A: country   B: people   C: time   D: river

3. _____ to our town enjoy our small museum.
   A: Stops   B: Riversides   C: Visitors   D: Buses

4. This old bridge is one of London's most famous _____.
   A: times   B: rivers   C: cities   D: sights

Reading

Choose the best answer.

1. (　) Why are river taxis like buses?
    A: They are both cheap.
    B: They both have wheels.
    C: They let people on and off at special stops.
    D: They both go along city streets.

2. (　) Visitors to Bangkok _____.
    A: rarely use river taxis
    B: like to swim in the Chao Praya River
    C: find river taxis are a good way to see the sights
    D: always save a lot of time

3. (　) What does "up and down" mean?
    A: in both directions   B: at all times
    C: around and around   D: in and out

4. (　) Which of the following is **not** true?
    A: River taxis are helpful to visitors.
    B: Driving in Bangkok can be difficult.
    C: There are rivers in many parts of Thailand.
    D: People get on and off river taxis anywhere along the riverside.

Grammar

Put the words in the correct order.

1. we   here   Can't   wait
   _____?

2. a   taxi   here   we   Can   get
   _____?

3. get   here   We   can't   off
   _____.

4 Weather Report

Currently (March 10) **Three-Day Forecast**

Boston

49° Cloudy

	Conditions	High/Low
Mon		51/38
Tue		50/35
Wed		45/33

New York

56° Partly Cloudy

	Conditions	High/Low
Mon		60/40
Tue		55/37
Wed		49/35

Baltimore

62° Sunny

	Conditions	High/Low
Mon		66/45
Tue		63/50
Wed		65/43

Vocabulary

Write the correct word in each blank.

| sunny | currently | forecast | cloudy | partly |

1. It's raining. The _____ for today's weather was wrong.

2. The sky is dark and _____. It might rain.

3. I'm _____ working at a department store.

4. You're _____ right, but not totally.

Reading

Choose the best answer.

1. (   ) On Tuesday, New York should be _____.
   - A: sunny
   - B: rainy
   - C: cloudy
   - D: partly cloudy

2. (   ) The high temperature on Wednesday for Baltimore is ____.
   - A: 62
   - B: 66
   - C: 65
   - D: 63

3. (   ) The weather report does **not** tell people about _____.
   - A: the high temperature
   - B: the humidity level
   - C: the weather conditions
   - D: the forecast for the next few days

4. (   ) Which day and place would be bad for hiking?
   - A: New York City on Wednesday.
   - B: Boston on Wednesday.
   - C: New York on Monday.
   - D: Baltimore on Tuesday.

Grammar

Put the words in the correct order.

1. it sunny in Boston Will be today

   _____?

2. partly going to be it Is cloudy

   _____?

3. might partly be tomorrow It sunny

   _____.

5 Trans-Canada Railroad

From the Atlantic Ocean to the Pacific Ocean, the Trans-Canada Railroad crosses Canada in style. For people who don't want __(1)__ drive or take a plane, taking a train is a good way to travel. It also __(2)__ a great vacation.

On a train, you can experience Canada's natural beauty. The railway crosses the Rocky Mountains. It also passes the lakes of Ontario and __(3)__ goes by Niagara Falls.

During the trip, you can rest for a day or two in interesting places like Montreal. You can even have your own private room and bathroom on the train. Now that's __(4)__!

Vocabulary

Choose the best answer.

1. This year, let's go on _____ to Mexico.
   A: vacation   B: room   C: place   D: ocean

2. This table is 100% _____. It's made of wood.
   A: interesting B: private   C: great   D: natural

3. I don't like to _____ by plane. I'm afraid of flying.
   A: travel   B: rest   C: experience   D: pass

4. Don't _____ the street here. It's not safe.
   A: take   B: cross   C: have   D: want

Reading

Choose the best answer.

1. ( ) A: for
        B: to
        C: a
        D: like

2. ( ) A: can be
        B: can do
        C: is being
        D: has

3. ( ) A: plus
        B: will
        C: can
        D: even

4. ( ) A: so uncomfortable
        B: traveling in style
        C: really crowded
        D: not possible in Canada

Grammar

Combine the two sentences into one sentence.

1. It's a good way to travel. Also, it's a great vacation.
   _____

2. You can see mountains. Also, you can see lakes.
   _____

3. It passes by Lake Ontario. Also, it passes by Niagara Falls.
   _____

6 Cold Soup

Vocabulary   Write the correct word in each blank.

| salty | certainly | customer | delicious | terrible |

1. That restaurant is famous. Its food is _____.

2. Can you help me fix my computer? _____.

3. I thought the music was good, but the acting was _____.

4. Sir, a _____ wants to talk to you about her dinner.

Reading

Choose the best answer.

1. ( ) The customer's soup _____.
    A: has too much sugar in it
    B: is hot enough to eat
    C: costs more than a bowl of vegetable soup
    D: has more than one problem

2. ( ) How does the waiter behave?
    A: Impatiently.   B: Strangely.
    C: Angrily.   D: Politely.

3. ( ) The waiter does **not** mention which kind of soup?
    A: Chicken noodle.   B: Tomato.
    C: Mushroom.   D: Vegetable.

4. ( ) The customer wants to exchange the bad soup for _____.
    A: another meal
    B: a bowl of vegetable soup
    C: a dessert
    D: a new bowl of the same kind of soup

Grammar

Match each question with the correct answer.

1. ___ How is your food?   A. A little more, thanks.

2. ___ Are you ready to order?   B. It's pasta, with soup and a drink.

3. ___ What's today's special?
                                    C. Everything's great.

4. ___ Would you like some more water?
                                    D. We need a few more minutes, please.

7 Venus and Serena Williams

Venus and Serena Williams are two very special sisters. They are two of the best women's tennis players in the world, and they win many tournaments every year. Often in the final match of a tournament, Venus and Serena play against each other. They are sisters and best friends, but they still try very hard to win.

Venus is older and taller than Serena, but Serena is extremely strong and fast. The sisters have different playing styles, but they both hit the ball very hard. With their speed and power, they are helping change the way women's tennis is played.

Vocabulary

Choose the best answer.

1. The car's _____ is too fast for this road.
   A: power   B: speed   C: wheel   D: tournament

2. What time does the next _____ start?
   A: style   B: tennis   C: ball   D: match

3. Many basketball players are _____ tall.
   A: each   B: extremely   C: many   D: quickly

4. We need to find some _____ people to lift this rock.
   A: fast   B: special   C: strong   D: final

Reading

Choose the best answer.

1. (　) Serena _____ Venus.
   A: is taller than　　　　　　B: always wins against
   C: is the same height as　　D: is younger than

2. (　) What does the article suggest about women's tennis?
   A: Speed and power are becoming more important.
   B: All the other players are strong and fast.
   C: More and more sisters are playing tennis together.
   D: Changes to the game have little to do with Venus and Serena.

3. (　) What is a "tournament"?
   A: A style of tennis.　　　B: A prize.
   C: A sporting contest.　　D: An amount of money.

4. (　) Which of the following is true?
   A: Venus and Serena don't play exactly the same way.
   B: The two sisters win every tournament.
   C: Venus and Serena rarely play each other.
   D: Only Venus hits the ball hard.

Grammar

Match the parts of the sentences.

1. ___ Both of them　　　　**A.** has great speed.

2. ___ One of them　　　　**B.** one of the tallest players.

3. ___ They are　　　　　　**C.** play well.

4. ___ She is　　　　　　　**D.** two of the best players.

8 The Last Day of the Last Class

Tammy, Linda, and Jennifer were best friends. They attended the same junior high school, senior high school, and even university together. The three friends had a nice custom. Every year, after the last day of class, they took a photograph together.

But all things, good and bad, must come to an end. After the last day of their final year of university, the three friends went to a photographer's studio. They took several pictures. It was the final year of their custom. They were a little sad, but they were happy to have so many good memories.

Vocabulary   Write the correct word in each blank.

| custom | attend | memories | university | final |

1. I have many nice _____ of living in England.

2. I did well on my _____ exams.

3. I hope you can _____ the meeting.

4. Do you plan to go to a _____ near your house?

Reading

Choose the best answer.

1. ( ) When did the friends take photos together?
   A: At the end of each school year.
   B: During winter vacation.
   C: Every day after class.
   D: Three times per year.

2. ( ) What was special about the friends' trip to the studio?
   A: It was their first time taking photographs together.
   B: The studio had special prices that day.
   C: The friends were happier than ever.
   D: The friends knew it was the end of their custom.

3. ( ) What does "attend" mean?
   A: go to   B: visit
   C: teach at   D: live near

4. ( ) Which of the following is true?
   A: The three friends first met each other in university.
   B: During high school, the friends didn't follow their custom.
   C: The friends took more than one photograph at the studio.
   D: The father of one of the friends owned a studio.

Grammar

Put the words in the correct order.

1. a lot of We took pictures
   _____.

2. had together a great They time
   _____.

3. of them were sad All little a
   _____.

4. attend Did they university the same
   _____?

9 Email: Summer Plans

To: jen351980@yahoo.com
From: skyflyer@hotmail.com
Subject: Summer Plans

Hi Jen,

Sorry for replying so late. I don't check my email very often. You know how busy things can get.

You asked about my summer plans. Good question! The truth is I really don't know. I want to take a few weeks off and go traveling. It would be wonderful to see you. But the way things are at work, that might be hard.

Oh, thanks for sending the photo of you and Ted. You look great together. I hope to meet him soon – maybe this summer. But that's a big maybe.

Anyway, I have to get back to work.

Take care,

Louise

Vocabulary

Choose the best answer.

1. Mario is a _____ piano player.
   A: wonderful   B: often   C: hard   D: late

2. After weeks of hard work, the police found out the _____ about the crime.
   A: question   B: truth   C: traveling   D: summer

3. I called you last night. _____ your telephone messages.
   A: Take off   B: Look   C: Plan   D: Check

4. Did Matthew ever _____ to your letter?
   A: hope   B: check   C: reply   D: meet

Reading

Choose the best answer.

1. (　) Who received the email?
   - A: Ted.
   - B: Jen.
   - C: Louise.
   - D: The boss.

2. (　) Louise wants to _____ during the summer.
   - A: stay home
   - B: get a job
   - C: take a trip
   - D: take some photos

3. (　) Louise thinks Ted and Jen _____.
   - A: shouldn't be together
   - B: should visit her
   - C: are a good couple
   - D: are too busy

4. (　) Which of the following is true?
   - A: The sender of the email doesn't have plans for the summer.
   - B: Louise met Ted last summer.
   - C: It's easy for Louise to take time off from work.
   - D: Louise asked Jen about her summer plans.

Grammar

Put the words in the correct order.

1. email didn't I my check

   _____.

2. ask my work about You didn't

   _____.

3. attach photo didn't You the

   _____.

4. She about plans tell didn't her me

   _____.

10 Castles

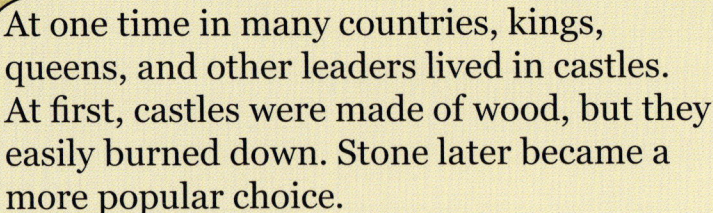

At one time in many countries, kings, queens, and other leaders lived in castles. At first, castles were made of wood, but they easily burned down. Stone later became a more popular choice.

Castles were often built on hills, to make them easier to defend. Large stone walls around the main buildings gave more protection. Most castles were small, but some, such as Windsor Castle in England, were very large. Castles were not usually comfortable places to live in, but that didn't matter. Their main purpose was to stop an enemy attack and protect the people inside.

Vocabulary

Write the correct word in each blank.

| stone | comfortable | attack | protect | enemy |

1. I love your new sofa. It's so _____.

2. Someone threw a big _____ through the window.

3. Umbrellas _____ people from the rain.

4. The cat is a famous _____ of the mouse.

Reading

Choose the best answer.

1. (   ) Why did stone become a more popular building choice?
    A: It was cheaper than wood.
    B: It didn't burn down as easily as wood.
    C: It looked better than wood.
    D: It was easier to find than wood.

2. (   ) Windsor Castle is an example of _____.
    A: a castle made of wood
    B: a castle on a hill
    C: a comfortable place to live
    D: a big castle

3. (   ) What does "defend" mean?
    A: see   B: attack
    C: build   D: protect

4. (   ) The article suggests that castles on flat ground _____.
    A: are less easy to defend than castles on a hill
    B: easily burn down
    C: all have large stone walls around them
    D: are easy to build

Grammar

Match the two parts of the sentences.

1. ___ They were built   A. by walls.

2. ___ They were made   B. by enemies.

3. ___ They were protected   C. on hills.

4. ___ They were attacked   D. of stone.

11 Express Your Opinion

What's your opinion about credit cards?

Carlos: I think they're great. I don't like carrying around a lot of cash, so I find credit cards very convenient.

Monique: In my opinion, they're dangerous. People aren't careful with their money, and they spend more than they should.

Terrance: The way I see it, they can be good or bad. We need to be responsible with credit cards. Otherwise, they can be a big problem.

Haruku: I love my credit cards! I use them all the time, for ordering movie tickets, buying things on-line, and renting DVDs. I can't imagine living without them.

Vocabulary

Choose the best answer.

1. Sometimes I like to _____ that I'm a king.
   A: imagine   B: order   C: spend   D: carry

2. My _____ about the subject is different from Julie's.
   A: problem   B: think   C: thing   D: opinion

3. Do you have enough _____ to buy the tickets?
   A: on-line   B: cash   C: credit cards   D: movies

4. People should be _____ for their own actions.
   A: bad   B: dangerous   C: convenient   D: responsible

Reading

Choose the best answer.

1. (　) Haruku thinks credit cards are _____.
    A: too dangerous
    B: sometimes good and sometimes bad
    C: very useful
    D: easy to live without

2. (　) Which two people have similar opinions about credit cards?
    A: Monique and Terrance.   B: Terrance and Haruku.
    C: Carlos and Monique.   D: Carlos and Haruku.

3. (　) Who has the most balanced opinion?
    A: Carlos.   B: Monique.
    C: Terrance.   D: Haruku.

4. (　) Which of the following is true?
    A: Each of the four people has a positive opinion of credit cards.
    B: None of the people own a credit card.
    C: Carlos prefers credit cards over cash.
    D: Terrance is not a responsible person.

Grammar

Write the correct form of each word.

1. Carlos _____ that they are convenient.
   (think/thinks)

2. I _____ think that I need one.
   (don't/no)

3. Do you _____ that you will spend a lot?
   (think/thinking)

4. She _____ think that they are dangerous.
   (don't/doesn't)

23

12 Credit Card Receipt

Vocabulary

Write the correct word in each blank.

| copy | receipt | signature | total | business |

1. Put your _____ on the last line of the form.

2. The _____ for the toys was $48.00.

3. To be good at _____, you need many different skills.

4. To return the broken television, bring it to the store along with the _____.

Reading

Choose the best answer.

1. (　) The customer used the credit card _____.
    A: in the morning   B: at night
    C: in the summer   D: in November

2. (　) What does the store sell?
    A: Credit cards.   B: Everything on the Internet.
    C: Toys.   D: We don't know.

3. (　) The receipt does **not** show _____.
    A: the customer's address
    B: the amount of money paid
    C: the customer's name
    D: the store's Internet address

4. (　) Which of the following is true?
    A: The store does not accept MasterCard, only Visa.
    B: The card expires about two years after the purchase date.
    C: The total price is more than $40.00.
    D: The credit card number is 12 numbers long.

Grammar

Write the correct form of each word.

1. The new _____ is very _____.
   (busy/business)   (busy/busily)

2. The card will _____ in 2009.
   (expire/expiration)

3. Please _____ the _____.
   (signature/sign)   (receive/receipt)

4. What _____ card do you have?
   (typical/type)

13 Journal

May 15

Well, it was a good and bad day. First, the bad news. At school, I had three exams. I probably did well on the math test, but I'm not so sure about history 101 and biology 10. After the third exam, I was really tired! But Mr. Lane told a few jokes, and we all laughed. He's so funny.

The good news is my package from Amazon.com arrived in the mail. It was my copy of the new Harry Potter book. It's really long, and I want to read it right away! Some of my friends already have it. Finally, I can read it too!

Vocabulary   Choose the best answer.

1. Tell us one of your funny _____.
   A: jokes   B: friends   C: news   D: copies

2. We might _____ at the party a little late.
   A: get   B: have   C: laugh   D: arrive

3. Look at the black sky. It's _____ going to rain soon.
   A: probably   B: after   C: already   D: well

4. Look, I got a _____ from my friend in India!
   A: mail   B: package   C: test   D: news

Reading

Choose the best answer.

1. (　) What made the writer tired?
   A: Listening to a joke.
   B: Reading a book.
   C: Waking up early.
   D: Taking several tests.

2. (　) How does the writer feel about the new Harry Potter book?
   A: Tired.   B: Excited.
   C: Hard.   D: Funny.

3. (　) What does "right away" mean?
   A: some time later   B: in the past
   C: the correct way   D: very soon

4. (　) What is true about the new Harry Potter book?
   A: Everybody has a copy.
   B: The writer bought several copies for her friends.
   C: It might take a long time to read.
   D: It's cheapest to buy it from Amazon.com.

Grammar

Put the words in the correct order.

1. had really I day great a
   _____.

2. the exam me told Mr. Lane passed I
   _____.

3. jokes laughed at a lot his I
   _____.

14 Superstitions

Lucky

At the end of every rainbow, you can find a pot of gold.

Finding a penny (1¢ or one cent coin) on the ground is good luck.

For good luck, hang a horseshoe on the wall above a door. Make sure the horseshoe is in a "u" shape.

Unlucky

Don't walk under a ladder. It brings bad luck.

It's bad to break a mirror. Doing so leads to seven years of bad luck.

Opening an umbrella inside a house is bad luck.

Vocabulary

Write the correct word in each blank.

| mirror | make sure | shape | hang | rainbow |

1. The sun and moon both have a round _____.

2. We can _____ the painting over there by the window.

3. The _____ only stayed in the sky for a few minutes.

4. _____ the door is completely closed.

Reading

Choose the best answer.

1. (　) To avoid bad luck, _____.
    - A: open an umbrella indoors
    - B: break a mirror
    - C: hang a horseshoe in an "n" shape
    - D: don't walk under a ladder

2. (　) Which of the following can bring good luck?
    - A: A mirror.
    - B: An umbrella.
    - C: A penny.
    - D: A ladder.

3. (　) What does "lead to" mean?
    - A: break
    - B: follow
    - C: bring
    - D: find

4. (　) Which of the following is true?
    - A: It's good luck to hang horseshoes above doors.
    - B: It's good luck to throw pennies on the ground.
    - C: It's bad luck to break an umbrella.
    - D: It's bad luck to walk next to a ladder.

Grammar

Match the two parts.

1. ___ Don't open an umbrella   A. my antique mirror.
2. ___ Don't walk   B. It's bad luck.
3. ___ Don't do that.   C. under a ladder.
4. ___ Please don't break   D. inside the house.

15 Disagreeing

Melissa: Our club is too small. We need to find a way to get more members.

Francisco: I disagree. ___(1)___ Why do you want more?

Melissa: Because bigger clubs are better. Other people always talk about how small our club ___(2)___.

Francisco: So what? I'm happy with the way things are. We're all good friends. In those big clubs, people don't know each other so well.

Melissa: That's not the way I see it. I know people in big clubs. ___(3)___

Francisco: Maybe we should take a vote ___(4)___ what to do.

Melissa: That's fair. Do you want to set it up?

Francisco: Sure. Everybody, listen up....

Vocabulary

Choose the best answer.

1. Why do I have to do everything? It's not _____.
   A: big   B: fair   C: well   D: up

2. All the _____ in our group are good friends.
   A: members   B: clubs   C: things   D: ones

3. I _____ with your opinion of Julie.
   A: vote   B: see   C: talk   D: disagree

4. Maybe you should _____ to the store manager.
   A: complain   B: decide   C: get   D: know

Reading

Choose the best answer.

1. (　) 　A: We need a lot more members.
　　　　B: Our club is not at all big.
　　　　C: We have plenty of people already.
　　　　D: I feel the same way as you do.

2. (　) 　A: being
　　　　B: is
　　　　C: it is
　　　　D: to be

3. (　) 　A: They don't get along very well.
　　　　B: They don't complain about that sort of thing.
　　　　C: They feel the same way as you.
　　　　D: They want to join smaller clubs.

4. (　) 　A: for decide
　　　　B: to deciding
　　　　C: decide
　　　　D: to decide

Grammar

Match the two statements.

1. ___ Do you agree?　　　　　　A: I am, too.

2. ___ I disagree.　　　　　　　B: Yes, I do.

3. ___ I'm voting "yes."　　　　C: I don't either.

4. ___ I don't agree.　　　　　　D: I do, too.

16 Kyoto

Located about 60 miles west of Tokyo (100 kilometers), Kyoto is one of Japan's most beautiful cities. Kyoto was once the capital of Japan. Now, besides being a cultural and business center, it is a very popular place to visit.

With its peaceful, tree-lined streets and quiet river paths, Kyoto is a great city to walk in. It's the home of many famous temples, like the Golden Temple. Some temples have rock gardens. They're carefully made with special designs. They give off a peaceful feeling. This feeling is also shown in the smiling faces of Kyoto's friendly people.

Vocabulary

Write the correct word in each blank.

| cultural | temple | peaceful | kilometers | capital |

1. Taking a walk by the ocean is very _____.

2. Hiroshima is about 100 _____ from here.

3. London is the _____ of England.

4. There's a small _____ not far from my house.

Reading

Choose the best answer.

1. (　) Where is Kyoto?
    A: Next to the capital of Japan.
    B: Somewhere east of Tokyo.
    C: In the center of Japan.
    D: About 100 kilometers away from Tokyo.

2. (　) Which words could describe Kyoto?
    A: Loud and busy.
    B: Crowded and unfriendly.
    C: Cold and modern.
    D: Calm and friendly.

3. (　) Which of the following is **not** discussed?
    A: The people of Kyoto.   B: Kyoto's museums.
    C: Rock gardens in Kyoto.   D: Kyoto's temples.

4. (　) What do we learn about Kyoto's temples?
    A: Many of them are famous.
    B: They all have rock gardens.
    C: They charge people money to go inside.
    D: Most of them have special designs.

Grammar

Combine the two sentences into one.

1. Shanghai is an interesting city. It is on the east coast of China.
   _____

2. Singapore is a small country. It is in Southeast Asia.
   _____

3. Beijing has many museums. One of them is the Natural History Museum.
   _____

4. Kyoto is a beautiful city. It is on the island of Honshu.
   _____

17 Music Sales

Vocabulary   Choose the best answer.

1. Classical _____ usually includes violins.
   A: sales   B: singers   C: music   D: songs

2. The sales _____ for July is down this year.
   A: number   B: total   C: sold   D: musical

3. We need to increase our _____ this year.
   A: CDs   B: number   C: music   D: sales

4. Popular music is also called _____.
   A: country   B: classic   C: pop   D: rock

Reading

Choose the best answer.

1. ( ) Country music sales made up _____ of the total sales.
   A: 8%   B: 13%
   C: 17% D: 20%

2. ( ) Which kind of music made up the highest percentage of sales?
   A: Classical   B: Country
   C: Pop   D: R&B

3. ( ) What was the sales amount of rock music?
   A: $20.00   B: $18,000
   C: $3,600   D: $9,000

4. ( ) What is the average price of each CD?
   A: $1.80
   B: $15.00
   C: $12.00
   D: $18.00

Grammar

Write the correct word in each blank.

1. The average _____ of a CD is $15.00.
   (amount/price)
2. What _____ of our sales was for rock?
   (percent/total)
3. We _____ a lot of CDs last month.
   (sell/sold)
4. She worked as a _____ person.
   (sale/sales)

18 Elephants

Elephants are very special animals. They are highly intelligent and show different emotions, such as happiness and sadness. They can even cry. Elephants can learn many things, and in some countries, they work carrying heavy items.

There are two species of elephants: African and Asian. African elephants are larger, with males weighing 7,000 kilograms or more. All elephants eat a lot – up to 300 kilograms of food per day. They live for around 60 years.

Unfortunately, the number of wild elephants is going down. Many are killed for their tusks. Governments and private groups are trying to protect them, but it's not easy.

Vocabulary

Write the correct word in each blank.

| wild | species | intelligent | heavy | emotion |

1. Many people say love is the most powerful _____.

2. This box is too _____ for me to lift.

3. I think a _____ animal went through our garbage last night.

4. How many _____ of birds live in this area?

Reading

Choose the best answer.

1. (　) How much food can elephants eat every day?
    A: 2 kilograms.　　　　B: 60 kilograms.
    C: 300 kilograms.　　　D: 7,000 kilograms.

2. (　) Which of these is an example of elephants' intelligence?
    A: They show different emotions.
    B: They can lift heavy things.
    C: They eat a lot.
    D: They can learn things.

3. (　) What is happening to wild elephants?
    A: They are very well protected.
    B: People are killing them to take their tusks.
    C: Their numbers are going up.
    D: They are becoming very popular in zoos.

4. (　) Which of the following is true?
    A: Asian elephants are smaller than African elephants.
    B: There are too many wild elephants in Africa.
    C: Everyone is trying to protect elephants.
    D: All elephants are the same size.

Grammar

Put the words in the correct order.

1. some　In　countries　work　they
   _____.

2. for　time　They　live　a　long
   _____.

3. from　hunters　We　them　protecting　are
   _____.

4. for　People　them　kill　tusks　their
   _____.

19 The Card Game

Every Friday evening, Matt plays cards with his friends. Four or five of them take part in the game. They meet at Matt's house at around 7:00 p.m. Each friend brings something to eat or drink, like snacks or soda.

After talking for a few minutes, they sit down to play. The game is fun and casual. Nobody is too serious, and nobody feels any pressure. The friends laugh and have a good time. Each card game lasts from two to three hours. It's an important event for each of the friends. It helps them relax and slow down their busy lives.

Vocabulary

Choose the best answer.

1. After school, my friends and I like to _____ at my house.
   A: relax   B: last   C: take part   D: help

2. You can wear _____ clothes to the party.
   A: important   B: busy   C: casual   D: each

3. Everybody at the office is feeling a lot of _____.
   A: events   B: pressure   C: lives   D: hours

4. Let's pick up some _____ at the supermarket.
   A: snacks   B: time   C: games   D: drink

Reading

Choose the best answer.

1. (　) The card game takes place _____.
    - A: every evening
    - B: in the morning
    - C: on the weekend
    - D: once a week

2. (　) Why is the card game important to the friends?
    - A: They need a chance to take a break.
    - B: They like to win money.
    - C: They need to show they are the best players.
    - D: They enjoy feeling pressure.

3. (　) Which word could describe the card game?
    - A: Serious.
    - B: Challenging.
    - C: Busy.
    - D: Relaxed.

4. (　) Which of the following is **not** true?
    - A: The card games are several hours long.
    - B: Matt provides all the snacks and drinks.
    - C: The game is in the evening.
    - D: The friends have fun during the game.

Grammar

Write the correct word in each blank.

We _____ last Friday to play cards. I _____
(met/meet)   (bring/brought)

some pizza. We _____ at Bill's jokes. Our game
                           (laughing/laughed)

_____ all night.
(lasts/lasted)

20 9 Ball

9 Ball is a very popular game. It's easy to learn and fun to play.

The game includes nine numbered balls and one white ball. First, the numbered balls are set up on one side of the table. Next, a player hits the white ball into the group of balls. The players then try to hit the numbered balls into any of the six pockets on the table (that's called "sinking" or "pocketing" a ball).

Players must sink the balls in order, starting with the 1 ball, then the 2 ball, and so on. The game is won by sinking the 9 ball.

Vocabulary

Write the correct word in each blank.

| easy | include | popular | set up | order |

1. Does the lunch special _____ a drink and dessert?

2. Many of my classmates love playing basketball. It's really _____.

3. What do we do next? I forget the correct _____.

4. Can you help me _____ the chairs before the concert?

Reading

Choose the best answer.

1. (　) Players try to hit _____.
   A: all the balls into the pockets at the same time
   B: only the 9 ball into a pocket
   C: the white ball into a pocket
   D: the numbered balls into the holes one by one

2. (　) What does the article suggest about 9 ball?
   A: You must have great skill to play it.
   B: Very few people enjoy playing the game.
   C: People have a good time playing it.
   D: It's expensive to play.

3. (　) What does "sinking" mean?
   A: Using the 9 ball to hit the other balls in.
   B: Hitting a ball into a pocket on the table.
   C: Setting up the numbered balls.
   D: Making a pocket in the table.

4. (　) What happens last in a game?
   A: Someone sinks the 9 ball.
   B: Someone sets up the numbered balls.
   C: Someone hits the numbered balls using the white ball.
   D: Someone sinks the 1 ball.

Grammar

Put the words in the correct order.

1. to　learn　game　easy　This　is
   _____.

2. to　win　always　nice　It　is
   _____.

3. to　play　think　is　it　I　fun
   _____.

4. to　hit　last　necessary　It　is　the　9 ball
   _____.

21 Flower Gardening

To plant a flower garden, you only need a few things: tools, seeds, and soil. People can grow many different flowers, such as roses and daisies. They all need water and light to grow, as well as daily attention.

The size of a garden isn't important. It may be in a large plot of land in a backyard. It might be in a meter-long box inside a house.

Gardening helps people relax and feel good about themselves. It's a wonderful feeling to take care of something and watch it grow. A garden is also a beautiful sight enjoyed by friends and relatives.

Vocabulary   Choose the best answer.

1. You should pay _____ to what the teacher is saying.
   A: feeling   B: sight   C: watching   D: attention

2. Your dog is so big! How did he _____ so quickly?
   A: grow   B: relax   C: plant   D: get

3. The young woman wore a _____ in her hair.
   A: water   B: garden   C: flower   D: seed

4. Eating three meals a day is part of many people's _____ life.
   A: daily   B: different   C: large   D: beautiful

Reading

Choose the best answer.

1. (　) The article suggests that without water and light _____.
   A: a garden only needs a lot of attention
   B: plants and flowers cannot grow
   C: people cannot buy seeds for a garden
   D: a garden needs to be large

2. (　) The article mentions roses and daisies to _____.
   A: talk about the most popular flowers
   B: suggest the best flowers for a garden
   C: give examples of two types of flowers for a garden
   D: show the importance of bright colors in a garden

3. (　) In the third sentence, "they" means _____.
   A: flowers   B: people
   C: seeds   D: roses

4. (　) Which benefit of gardening is not mentioned?
   A: Helping you relax.
   B: Giving you a good feeling.
   C: Growing flowers to sell.
   D: Sharing a thing of beauty with others.

Grammar

Complete each sentence with *a few, much,* or *a lot of.*

1. There are _____ spiders in your yard! Hundreds!

2. How _____ water do plants need?

3. Plant only _____ seeds.

4. There are _____ flowers everywhere inside her house.

22 Seeing a Doctor

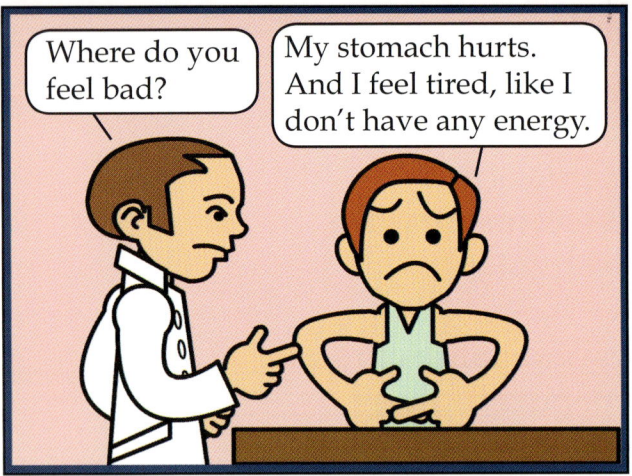

Vocabulary

Write the correct word in each blank.

| medicine | spicy | stomach | definitely | careful |

1. Eating all that ice cream gave me _____ pains.

2. Thai food is good, but it's so _____.

3. I took some _____ this morning, so I'm a little tired now.

4. Greg gets angry easily. Be _____ what you say to him.

Reading

Choose the best answer.

1. ( ) The patient's problem started _____.
   A: before dinner
   B: a week ago
   C: in the morning
   D: after a meal

2. ( ) What does the doctor think is wrong?
   A: The patient has a high fever.
   B: The patient has a cold.
   C: The patient ate too much spicy food.
   D: The patient ate some unclean or unhealthy food.

3. ( ) The doctor gives the patient _____.
   A: spicy food   B: medicine
   C: rest   D: a fever

4. ( ) What is the patient going to avoid?
   A: Spicy food.   B: All food.
   C: His medicine.   D: A day or two of rest.

Grammar

Match each question with the correct answer.

1. ___ What's the problem?   A. My stomach also hurts.

2. ___ When did it start?   B. My head hurts.

3. ___ Is anything else the matter?   C. No, I'm not.

4. ___ Are you taking any medicine?   D. Some time last night.

23 Personal Website

http://www.ourbigbluemarble.com

Our Big Blue Marble

About Me

Photos

Links

Guestbook

Email me

Welcome to my website! You're probably wondering about the site's name: Our Big Blue Marble. Well, some people say the Earth looks like a big blue marble. So, I thought it was a cool name for a site! To visit the different parts of the site, click on one of the links to the left.

Please remember to sign my Guestbook!

Recent updates:

7/15 - Photos from my trip to France added!
8/28 - New section: Links to other cool sites
9/10 - More interesting things about me added

Vocabulary

Write the correct word in each blank.

1. Did you _____ to feed the cat?
   A: click   B: remember   C: pet   D: welcome

2. My friend sent me a _____ to a really cool website.
   A: guestbook   B: section   C: photo   D: link

3. I try to _____ new things to my website every week.
   A: add   B: wonder   C: think   D: find

4. Check out my site again. There are a lot of new _____.
   A: marbles   B: emails   C: updates   D: ones

Reading

Choose the best answer.

1. (　) Where can you find a link to the Photos section of the site?
   A: At the top of the page.
   B: At the bottom of the page.
   C: On the left-hand side of the page.
   D: On the right-hand side of the page.

2. (　) "Big blue marble" is another name for _____.
   A: the creator of the website
   B: a section of the website
   C: the Earth
   D: a recent update

3. (　) What did the author add in July, 2003?
   A: Some interesting personal information.
   B: More links to other sites.
   C: Information about the Earth.
   D: Photos from a vacation.

4. (　) The website does **not** have a section with _____.
   A: a chatroom   B: a guestbook
   C: photos   D: links

Grammar

Put the words in the correct order.

1. like The a marble blue big is Earth
   _____.

2. guestbook sign my Please personal
   _____.

3. website parts has My different many
   _____.

4. you know cool website another Do
   _____?

24 Old Friends

Mr. Farlini and Mr. Costa are very old friends. They ___(1)___ more than 50 years ago, grew up in the same area, and were classmates through high school.

Every Tuesday, they get together at Antonio's Corner Coffee Shop in Newark, New Jersey. Each gentleman wears a suit. After long careers as businessmen, they ___(2)___ dressing formally.

The two old friends have a lot to talk about. Being friends for so long, they ___(3)___. Sometimes they play backgammon. At other times they look at old photographs. Sometimes they don't say or do anything at all. ___(4)___, they enjoy spending time together.

Vocabulary

Write the correct word in each blank.

| formally | gentleman | suit | chess | area |

1. There are a lot of good pizza shops in this _____.

2. After the meeting, people _____ shook hands with one another.

3. Josh has to wear a _____ to work every day.

4. Stand aside and let this _____ pass by.

Reading

Choose the best answer.

1. (　)　A: meeting
B: to meet
C: meet
D: met

2. (　)　A: are used to
B: used to
C: use to
D: are use to

3. (　)　A: don't know each other very well
B: are not very familiar with each other
C: have few common interests
D: know almost everything about one another

4. (　)　A: The most important
B: Most important
C: Too important
D: Being the most important

Grammar

Put the words in the correct order.

1. at work to night used I

   _____.

2. used businessmen They to be

   _____.

3. not used to weather cold I'm the

   _____.

25 Tai Shan

Tai Shan is one of China's five sacred mountains. People have great respect for the mountain, and there are many poems and stories about it. Every year, thousands of visitors travel to Shan Dong province to make the hike up.

The hike takes about one day, and the view along the way is beautiful. At the top are places to sleep and a large temple. An old tradition is to wake up early to watch the sun rise. The wind can be strong and cold, so people often wear heavy clothing. Watching the sun rise in such a beautiful place is a special experience.

Vocabulary

Choose the best answer.

1. The _____ of the beach from the hotel room is great!
   A: top   B: story   C: sand   D: view

2. I have a lot of _____ for hard-working people.
   A: experience   B: province   C: respect   D: temple

3. Do you want to read my _____ about winter?
   A: poem   B: clothing   C: weather   D: mountain

4. It was a bad _____, and I'm trying to forget it.
   A: experience   B: visitor   C: clothing   D: rise

Reading

Choose the best answer.

1. (　) Visitors to Tai Shan _____.
   A: are from Shan Dong
   B: stay at the temple
   C: sometimes write about the mountain
   D: always watch the sun rise

2. (　) Why do people wear heavy clothing early in the morning?
   A: There are many dangerous, sharp rocks.
   B: Wild animals run around the top of the mountain.
   C: The sunshine is very strong.
   D: The weather is sometimes bad.

3. (　) What can we infer about China's other sacred mountains?
   A: There are no poems or stories about them.
   B: People hold them in great respect.
   C: They are all in Shan Dong province.
   D: Most of them are taller than Tai Shan.

4. (　) Which of the following is true?
   A: It takes about two days to hike up Tai Shan.
   B: There isn't much to see on the way up the mountain.
   C: Only a few people may go up Tai Shan each year.
   D: Tai Shan is in Shan Dong province.

Grammar

Match the two parts of the sentences.

1. ___ The wind		A. is sacred.
2. ___ The mountain		B. is heavy.
3. ___ The view		C. is strong.
4. ___ Their clothing		D. is beautiful.

26 Magazine Cover

Vocabulary

Write the correct word in each blank.

| pet | perfect | dream | conversation | fashion |

1. A few days ago, I had a long _____ with Bob about baseball.

2. I want to get a _____ mouse or snake.

3. As a child, I used to _____ about being a firefighter.

4. I got a _____ score on my science test!

Reading

Choose the best answer.

1. ( ) The magazine is for _____ readers.
   A: old B: serious
   C: young D: perfect

2. ( ) The magazine has more than one article about _____.
   A: business
   B: Canada
   C: animals
   D: clothes

3. ( ) What does "come true" mean?
   A: go somewhere
   B: wake up
   C: come out
   D: become real

4. ( ) The cover does **not** show _____.
   A: prices for two places
   B: the date of the issue
   C: the titles of several articles
   D: the number of pages in the magazine

Grammar

Combine the two sentences into one sentence.

1. It's a new magazine with a lot of articles. The articles are about fashion.

   _____

2. It's a monthly magazine. It's for young people.

   _____

3. Here's a beautiful photograph. It's from a fashion magazine.

   _____

27 Habits

Habits are an important part of our lives. They affect a lot of our daily actions, like the time we go to sleep, the things we eat, and even the way we behave. Such habits can be helpful. They save us time and energy. We don't have to think hard about every small decision.

It's easy to form habits, but it can be very hard to break them. Many people have bad habits, like sleeping too much, eating junk food, and so on. First, we need to be aware of our bad habits. Then, we can start to change them.

Vocabulary Choose the best answer.

1. We need to make a _____ about this case.
   A: habit   B: life   C: action   D: decision

2. Sit down. Don't _____ like a monkey.
   A: behave   B: change   C: break   D: save

3. Are you _____ of the noise your car is making?
   A: helpful   B: loud   C: aware   D: important

4. Sometimes, the weather can _____ my mood.
   A: affect   B: think   C: be   D: rain

Reading

Choose the best answer.

1. (　) According to the article, _____ habits.
    A: few people have
    B: it's impossible to change
    C: there are good and bad
    D: we need to break all of our

2. (　) How can habits be helpful?
    A: They always help us make the right decisions.
    B: They save us time.
    C: They make us behave like better people.
    D: They let us sleep too much.

3. (　) Why does the article mention eating junk food?
    A: To give an example of healthy things to eat.
    B: To give an example of a good habit.
    C: To give an example of how to change ourselves.
    D: To give an example of a bad habit.

4. (　) What is another way to say "be aware of"?
    A: break   B: recognize
    C: form   D: forget

Grammar

Write the correct word.

It's easy to _____ habits, but _____ to change
　　　　　　　(break/form)　　　　　　　　　(hard/hardly)

them. We should look _____ at our behavior and
　　　　　　　　　　　　(careful/carefully)

_____ our bad habits such as eating too _____.
(start/change)　　　　　　　　　　　　　　　　　　　　　　(fast/fastly)

28 Instant Message

Instant Message

Now talking with: Sunshine

Heidi: Good morning, Sunshine.

Sunshine: Hey, what's up?

Heidi: Not too much. I was just checking out a cool site. Take a look: www.flashmagicaction.com

Sunshine: OK, thanks. Oh, I bought a few CDs on Ebay today. :)

Heidi: Excellent. I use the site a lot for buying CDs and DVDs. Prices are sometimes really good.

Sunshine: Right, but you need to be careful. Some people may try to cheat you.

Font   Color   **B**   *I*   :)

That's true. Some sellers aren't honest.   [Send]

Vocabulary

Write the correct word in each blank.

| price | seller | cheat | honest | excellent |

1. Unfortunately, some people in the world like to _____ others.

2. You did an _____ job on your book report.

3. Excuse me, what's the _____ of this computer?

4. Always be _____, and don't tell lies.

Reading

Choose the best answer.

1. (　) Heidi wants Sunshine to _____.
    - A: buy something on-line
    - B: help her buy something
    - C: visit a website
    - D: listen to a CD

2. (　) What do both Heidi and Sunshine like to buy on Ebay?
    - A: DVDs.
    - B: Websites.
    - C: CDs.
    - D: Books.

3. (　) What does "check out" mean?
    - A: set up
    - B: look at
    - C: take away
    - D: buy from

4. (　) Sunshine and Heidi both feel _____.
    - A: flashmagicaction.com is a cool site
    - B: everybody on-line is honest
    - C: Ebay is the best site on the Internet
    - D: there are dishonest sellers on Ebay

Grammar

Match each question with the correct answer.

1. ___ What's up?	**A.**	A part for my car.
2. ___ What did you buy?	**B.**	In a few minutes.
3. ___ When did you get here?	**C.**	You know – the same as always.
4. ___ When are you leaving?	**D.**	About an hour ago.

29 Profile of an English Teacher

Vicki Callagan teaches English at Pierce College, in Tacoma, Washington. She started teaching more than 25 years ago. After all this time, she still loves her job.

Vicki likes using a special activity in her classes. She makes videos with her students. The activity is a good way for the students to improve language skills. Plus, everyone has a great time!

In her free time, Vicki enjoys being with her husband and two children. They like outdoor activities such as skiing and kayaking. Of course, on every trip, Vicki makes videos of her family and the places they visit.

Vocabulary   Choose the best answer.

1. We should take a _____ to South America this year.
   A: video   B: trip   C: husband   D: job

2. Keeping a diary is a great way to _____ your writing.
   A: make   B: visit   C: teach   D: improve

3. Every student in the class can be part of the speaking _____.
   A: activity   B: family   C: year   D: skill

4. Kayaking is a(n) _____ activity.
   A: often   B: outdoor   C: special   D: skiing

Reading

Choose the best answer.

1. (   ) Vicki feels her job is _____.
   - A: old
   - B: boring
   - C: enjoyable
   - D: easy

2. (   ) For fun, Vicki likes to _____.
   - A: build kayaks
   - B: take trips with her students
   - C: make videos
   - D: improve her language skills

3. (   ) Why does Vicki make videos with her students?
   - A: It's cheaper than watching movies in theaters.
   - B: Making videos is an important skill.
   - C: It helps students improve their English.
   - D: It's the best way to pass the time.

4. (   ) Which of the following is true?
   - A: Vicki has more than 20 years of teaching experience.
   - B: Vicki makes videos only at her school.
   - C: Vicki teaches at a high school.
   - D: Vicki uses only books to teach her classes.

Grammar

Write the past tense form of each verb.

1. My husband _____ (teach) at a high school.

2. We _____ (buy) a kayak.

3. I _____ (think) that you went skiing yesterday.

4. George _____ (catch) a bad cold during his trip to the mountains.

30 Music of Korea: The Changgo

The changgo is a large drum used in many kinds of Korean music, such as traditional songs and dance music. The changgo has an interesting shape, like an hourglass. Its body is made from one large piece of wood. Sometimes players carry the changgo, but they usually sit down to play it.

There are leather heads on each side of the changgo. Ropes are used to tie them to the body. The player uses his hand to beat the left-hand side. A bamboo stick is used to beat the right-hand side. Striking the changgo in these different ways makes different sounds.

Vocabulary

Write the correct word in each blank.

| tie | interesting | wood | carry | leather |

1. Many old houses are made of _____.

2. I think traditional dances are really _____.

3. _____ your shoes, or you might fall down.

4. Can you _____ these books up the stairs for me?

Reading

Choose the best answer.

1. (　) How does a changgo player beat the left-hand side of the changgo?
   A: With a stick.　　　　　　　B: With a rope.
   C: With a piece of leather.　　D: With his hand.

2. (　) Beating the left and right-hand sides of the changgo _____ _____.
   A: sounds the same
   B: makes no difference
   C: makes different sounds
   D: is not a common way to play the changgo

3. (　) What does "beat" mean?
   A: kill　　　　B: make
   C: tie　　　　D: strike

4. (　) Which of the following is true about the changgo?
   A: The heads are made of wood.
   B: One piece of wood is used to make the body.
   C: Usually, players carry it around.
   D: The heads are not tied to the body.

Grammar

Write the correct word in the blank.

1. The stick _____ to hit the drum.
   (used/is used)

2. Both hands _____ with this drum.
   (used/are used)

3. Some music _____ a lot of drums.
   (uses/is used)

4. The musician _____ only traditional music.
   (used/is used)

31 Modern Heroes

Police officers and firefighters are our modern heroes. They work ___(1)___, on weekends and holidays, to keep our cities and towns safe. They protect us and our property, and they are the first people to arrive ___(2)___ an emergency.

It takes a brave man or woman to do such a hard job. It's dangerous work. ___(3)___ a fire is not an easy or safe thing to do. Neither is catching a thief. But somebody must do it. So the next time you see one of these modern heroes, ___(4)___. Tell them you appreciate their hard work.

Vocabulary   Choose the best answer.

1. Don't climb the wall like that. It's _____.
   A: safe   B: modern   C: dangerous   D: hard

2. The cat is running away. Quick, _____ it!
   A: catch   B: see   C: do   D: keep

3. Thank you very much. I _____ your help.
   A: protect   B: arrive   C: put out   D: appreciate

4. Let's do something together this _____.
   A: weekend   B: work   C: city   D: thing

Reading

Choose the best answer.

1. (　)　A: day to the night
        B: day then night
        C: day plus night
        D: day and night

2. (　)　A: with
        B: from
        C: by
        D: at

3. (　)　A: Put out
        B: Putting out
        C: Out putting
        D: To putting out

4. (　)　A: run away
        B: say goodbye
        C: thank them
        D: cry out

Grammar

Write the correct word or words in each blank.

1. Did they _____ the thief?
   (caught/catch)

2. Did they _____ on time.
   (arrive/to arrive)

3. We didn't _____ last weekend.
   (work/worked)

4. When did they _____ the fire?
   (out put/put out)

32 Making a Cheese Sandwich

1. First, prepare the ingredients: bread, cheese, lettuce, tomatoes, green peppers, and mustard (or another sauce).

2. Chop the vegetables into small pieces. Cut the bread into 1/3 inch slices and the cheese into 1/16 inch slices (if they are not pre-sliced).

3. On one piece of bread, add the vegetables, starting with the lettuce, then the tomatoes, and then the green peppers. Next, add one or two slices of cheese.

4. On the other piece of bread, add your sauce (mustard or mayonnaise are good choices). Put the two halves of the sandwich together. Enjoy!

Vocabulary

Write the correct word in each blank.

| ingredients | prepare | chop | enjoy | vegetable |

1. Would you like a bowl of _____ soup?

2. Please _____ the tomatoes in half.

3. Here are your tickets. _____ the concert.

4. Salt and pepper are two of the _____ for the pasta dish.

Reading

Choose the best answer.

1. (   ) Which of the following comes first?
    A: Put the two halves of the sandwich together.
    B: Chop up the vegetables.
    C: Put the vegetables on one piece of bread.
    D: Add the cheese.

2. (   ) How thick should each slice of bread be?
    A: 1/32 inch.   B: 1/16 inch.
    C: 1/3 inch.   D: 2 inches.

3. (   ) How many different ingredients are needed?
    A: Fewer than three.
    B: Six.
    C: About ten.
    D: At least twelve.

4. (   ) After the green peppers, add the _____.
    A: lettuce   B: bread
    C: cheese   D: tomatoes

Grammar

Put the words in the correct order.

1. into lettuce pieces Cut small the

   _____.

2. much Don't mustard use too

   _____.

3. you of kind What like do sauce

   _____?

33 Summer Music Festival

July Program Guide

Monday	Tuesday	Wednesday	Thursday	Friday	Saturday	Sunday
	1	2	3	4	5	6
	6:30 PM Traditional music from Spain			7:30 PM Rock music from the 1960's	2:00 PM Children's music from around the world	
7	8	9	10	11	12	13
		7:00 PM Dance party in the park. Food, drinks, and fun!			3:00 PM Free guitar lessons	2:00 PM A taste of Chinese opera
14	15	16	17	18	19	20
	6:00 PM African drums and dancing		8:00 PM Flute and piano concert		1:30 PM Karaoke party!	

Vocabulary

Choose the best answer.

1. After just a few _____, Jenny plays very well.
   A: parties   B: guitars   C: programs   D: lessons

2. Can I have a _____ of your cookie?
   A: drum   B: taste   C: guide   D: flute

3. Today's newspaper has a _____ to the summer movies.
   A: guide   B: party   C: show   D: fun

4. The _____ was great! Three different bands played.
   A: dancing   B: instrument   C: concert   D: taste

Reading

Choose the best answer.

1. (　) When is the dance party?
    - A: July 1st.
    - B: July 9th.
    - C: July 16th.
    - D: July 19th.

2. (　) For the third event of the month, _____.
    - A: there is a Chinese opera
    - B: people can receive free guitar lessons
    - C: there is a flute and piano concert
    - D: there is a program of children's music

3. (　) Daisy likes African and Asian music. She only has free time on weekends. What date is best for her?
    - A: July 1st.
    - B: July 9th.
    - C: July 13th.
    - D: July 15th.

4. (　) Which of the following is **not** true?
    - A: The Karaoke party is on a Saturday.
    - B: There are nine events per week.
    - C: There is music from Europe.
    - D: There are no events on Monday.

Grammar

Write the correct word in each blank.

1. There are concerts at the club _____ Saturday night.
   (per/every)

2. _____ person needs to have a ticket.
   (Each/All)

3. The cost is 50 dollars _____ ticket.
   (per/the)

4. Do _____ concerts begin at 8:00?
   (all/every)

34 Great Zimbabwe

Almost 1000 years ago, the city of Great Zimbabwe was the center of a powerful African state. Great Zimbabwe was a large city of at least 15,000 people. Surrounding the city were large, thick walls. They were very well made, and many of them still stand today.

The city became rich through gold mining. For almost 400 years, it traded with people in Africa, the Middle East, China, and elsewhere.

Great Zimbabwe was very important in the history of Southern Africa. In fact, the modern country of Zimbabwe takes its name from the ancient city.

Vocabulary

Write the correct word in each blank.

| ancient | powerful | rich | thick | trade |

1. Mr. Yan is _____. He has three or four cars.

2. In museums, you can see many _____ works of art.

3. Would you like to _____ your wallet for my watch?

4. The glass is _____, so we don't hear any noise from outside.

Reading

Choose the best answer.

1. (　) What is the main idea?
   A: Gold mining was important in international trade 400 years ago.
   B: The quality of buildings in Africa's old cities was high.
   C: Great Zimbabwe is an important part of Africa's ancient past.
   D: Cities of Southern Africa traded with China.

2. (　) The walls of Great Zimbabwe _____.
   A: did not easily fall down   B: were not well made
   C: were made 400 years ago   D: lasted less than 400 years

3. (　) The article does **not** mention which trading area?
   A: Europe.   B: Asia.
   C: Africa.   D: The Middle East.

4. (　) What does the article suggest?
   A: Cities in the Middle East mined gold.
   B: More than 20,000 people could live in Great Zimbabwe.
   C: There are thick walls around modern African cities.
   D: Gold was important in helping Great Zimbabwe become rich.

Grammar

Match the two phrases.

1. ___ 900   A. almost 400
2. ___ over 400   B. at least 1000
3. ___ 390   C. more than 400
4. ___ over 1000   D. almost 1000

35 Asking for Advice

Theresa: Bill, I need your advice.
Bill: Sure, what's up?
Theresa: OK, well, I'm friends with Lisa and Ashley. Lisa told me a huge secret, but I think Ashley should know. Should I tell her?
Bill: Is the secret about Ashley?
Theresa: Well, kind of. But I can't say too much about it.
Bill: I understand. Let me think…. On the one hand, it is a secret, and you shouldn't tell other people. But on the other hand, it's something about your good friend, and you want to help her. Maybe you should go see Lisa. Then the two of you can talk to Ashley together.
Theresa: Hey, good idea! Thanks!
Bill: Sure thing. I hope everything works out.

Vocabulary

Choose the best answer.

1. Do you want to study for the test _____?
   A: together   B: everything   C: other   D: should

2. She spoke Spanish, so I didn't _____ her.
   A: hope   B: listen   C: think   D: understand

3. Elephants are _____ animals.
   A: alone   B: tiny   C: sure   D: huge

4. Come here. I want to tell you a _____.
   A: thing   B: secret   C: something   D: friend

Reading

Choose the best answer.

1. (　) Bill is friends with _____.
   A: Ashley   B: Theresa
   C: Lisa   D: everybody

2. (　) What does Bill think about secrets?
   A: It's all right to tell them to anybody.
   B: We should tell secrets to most of our friends.
   C: People shouldn't carelessly tell them to other people.
   D: Nobody has secrets in today's world.

3. (　) What does "work out" mean?
   A: find out   B: be solved
   C: get strong   D: go away

4. (　) What is Theresa probably going to do?
   A: Talk to Lisa about seeing Ashley.
   B: Tell Ashley the secret.
   C: Tell Bill the secret.
   D: Ask Bill to tell her a secret.

Grammar

Put the words in the correct order.

1. I do What should

   _____?

2. her I tell Should

   _____?

3. a secret keep Should we it

   _____?

4. think I her tell should we

   _____.

36 Falling Rain

Falling Rain

I like the sound of falling rain –
Like music played on empty streets:
A concert on a summer's day,
Soft tapping with a gentle beat.

On rainy days I close my eyes
And smell the freshly blowing air.
It calms me down and gives me hope –
Enough to forget all my fear.

On rainy days, I look outside.
The streets are quiet, calm, and plain.
Is everyone else like me – inside,
Listening to the falling rain?

Vocabulary

Write the correct word in each blank.

| empty | blow | gently | forget | calm down |

1. Don't _____ to call your boss later on.

2. The soup is hot. _____ on it to cool it down.

3. It's Saturday afternoon. Why are all the stores _____?

4. The cat is very young. Pet it _____.

Reading

Choose the best answer.

1. (　) The writer compares the rain to _____.
   A: a street   B: everyone else
   C: music   D: the summer

2. (　) On rainy days, the writer _____.
   A: stays inside
   B: goes outside
   C: walks around
   D: plays music

3. (　) How does the rain make the writer feel?
   A: Nervous.   B: Calm.
   C: Worried.   D: Sad.

4. (　) What is fresh during the rain?
   A: The streets.
   B: The water.
   C: The city.
   D: The wind.

Grammar

Write the correct form of each word.

1. The rain is falling _____ (quiet/quietly).

2. The streets are _____ (calm/calmly).

3. The music is playing _____ (gentle/gently).

4. The air is very _____ (fresh/freshly).

37 Persian Rugs

Persian rugs are beautiful, traditional floor coverings. In the Middle East, South Asia, and East Asia, rug making is an art form going back hundreds of years. Different parts of the world are famous for using special materials, colors, and designs in their rugs.

The best rugs are handmade, usually from wool, using a machine called a loom. Some rugs are made from silk, and they can be very expensive.

High quality rugs are both beautiful and useful. They can last a long time. In fact, well-cared-for rugs can last a hundred years or longer.

Vocabulary

Choose the best answer.

1. What kind of _____ is your shirt made of?
   A: rug   B: material   C: color   D: part

2. Clothes from Italy are _____ around the world.
   A: well   B: famous   C: traditional   D: called

3. Don't buy that cheap television. The _____ is bad.
   A: time   B: silk   C: wool   D: quality

4. My computer is a very useful _____.
   A: machine   B: design   C: material   D: world

Reading

Choose the best answer.

1. (　) Why are high quality rugs good to own?
   A: They are more beautiful than cheap rugs.
   B: They always last hundreds of years.
   C: They are made of wool.
   D: They can be used for many years.

2. (　) In different parts of the world, _____.
   A: rugs are all the same
   B: only the designs and colors of rugs are different
   C: rugs are made in a variety of styles
   D: rugs are the most special things in people's houses

3. (　) What does "going back hundreds of years" mean?
   A: ending 200 or 300 years ago
   B: worth a lot of money for a long time
   C: made long ago
   D: starting hundreds of years ago

4. (　) What do people do with a loom?
   A: They make rugs.　　B: They make floors.
   C: They make wool.　　D: They make machines.

Grammar

Combine the two sentences into one sentence.

1. She has some beautiful rugs. They are from this village.

   _____

2. These rugs are handmade. They are made in small villages.

   _____

3. I want to buy the silk rug. It is in that shop.

   _____

38 Safe Driving

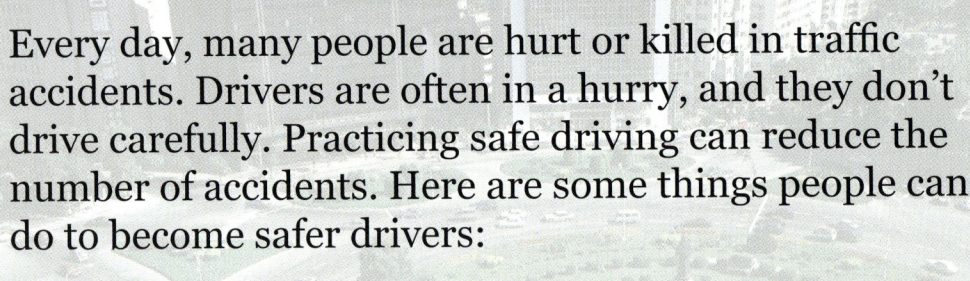

Every day, many people are hurt or killed in traffic accidents. Drivers are often in a hurry, and they don't drive carefully. Practicing safe driving can reduce the number of accidents. Here are some things people can do to become safer drivers:

1. Slow down.   High speeds cause a large number of accidents.
2. Be patient.   Don't get angry with other drivers.
3. Be polite.   Let other cars go ahead of you.
4. Be careful.   Watch for people crossing the street.

Remember, safe driving is not just about obeying the law. It's about saving lives.

Vocabulary

Choose the best answer.

1. The noisy child doesn't _____ his parents or teachers.
   A: practice   B: save   C: obey   D: watch

2. This is a dangerous road. There are _____ here every day.
   A: people   B: speeds   C: drivers   D: accidents

3. I don't know what is _____ the problems with my car.
   A: causing   B: hurting   C: becoming   D: getting

4. You may need to wait a few hours. Please be _____.
   A: polite   B: careful   C: angry   D: patient

Reading

Choose the best answer.

1. (　) According to the article, what causes a lot of accidents?
   A: People walking in the street.
   B: Drivers going too slowly.
   C: People driving carelessly.
   D: Drivers obeying the traffic laws.

2. (　) What does "reduce" mean?
   A: make lower
   B: put down
   C: make disappear
   D: pull in

3. (　) What does the article suggest is the most important reason to drive safely?
   A: It's the law.
   B: It saves lives.
   C: It saves time.
   D: It keeps the roads clean.

4. (　) What of the following safety tips is **not** mentioned?
   A: Checking the mirror often.
   B: Driving at a safe speed.
   C: Paying attention to people on foot.
   D: Showing kindness towards other drivers.

Grammar

Put the words in the correct order.

1. accident The caused speeding by was
   _____.

2. each people Many are killed year
   _____.

3. in accident people Five hurt were the
   _____.

4. accidents of number The was reduced
   _____.

39 Sign Language

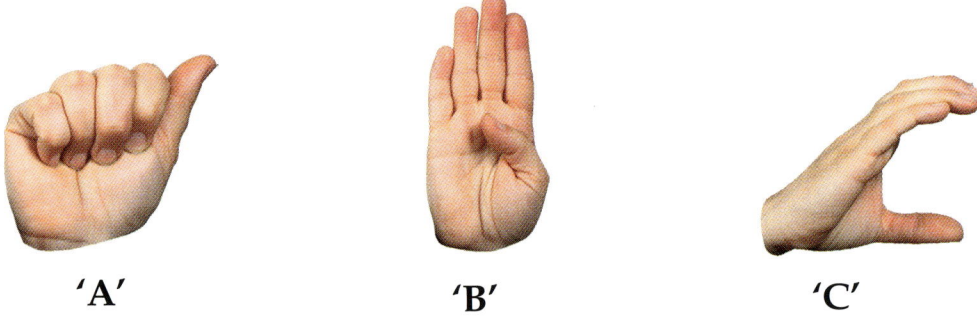

'A'   'B'   'C'

Deaf people use sign language to communicate with each other and with non-deaf people. There are hundreds of different sign languages around the world. They are like spoken languages, with their own vocabulary and systems of grammar. Many schools for the deaf use sign language in class.

Signs are made by making shapes with one's hands. A sign may include moving the hands or pointing in a certain direction. For example, in American Sign Language, to say "smart," touch your forehead with your middle finger and move it down and away. In some languages, the expressions on a signer's face can change the meaning of the sign.

Vocabulary

Choose the best answer.

1. Why do you have such a strange _____ on your face?
   A: direction   B: sign   C: grammar   D: expression
2. Some people can _____ with gorillas and other animals.
   A: say   B: make   C: point   D: communicate
3. I want to learn sign language to talk with my _____ friend.
   A: certain   B: different   C: deaf   D: loud
4. Teacher, I don't understand the _____ of this sentence.
   A: meaning   B: shape   C: face   D: line

Reading

Choose the best answer.

1. (　) How are signs made?
   A: With a person's mouth.　　B: With a person's eyes.
   C: With a person's forehead.　D: With a person's hands.

2. (　) How are sign languages similar to spoken languages?
   A: They both use signs made by a person's hands.
   B: They both have their own rules and vocabulary words.
   C: They both have exactly the same kinds of grammar.
   D: They are both used in every school around the world.

3. (　) What is another way to say "for example"?
   A: for instance　　　　B: in example
   C: in such way　　　　D: for a show

4. (　) Why are a person's expressions important in some sign languages?
   A: They can change a person's face.
   B: They can change a sign's meaning.
   C: They can change the shape of a person's hands.
   D: They can change the grammar of a sign language.

Grammar

Put the words in the correct order.

1. with　talk　They　hands　their
   _____.

2. with　a　language　grammar　It's　a
   _____.

3. with　finger　at　your　head　Point　your
   _____.

4. with　Can　deaf　communicate　people　non-deaf　people
   _____?

40 Global Positioning System

In the past, being lost could be big trouble. Car drivers had a hard time driving in new areas. Airplane pilots had trouble flying in bad weather. With the GPS, we can help solve such problems.

The GPS consists of 24 satellites in space, about 20,000 kilometers above the Earth. These satellites can tell an airplane or car exactly where it is. Even hikers can figure out their location using special GPS devices, and there are many other uses, too. The world is a big place, but the GPS makes it a lot easier to go from A to B.

Vocabulary

Write the correct word in each blank.

| trouble | weather | solve | exactly | location |

1. High up in the mountains, the _____ can get very cold.

2. Do you know the _____ of the hotel?

3. Calm down and tell me _____ what happened.

4. Some problems are very hard to _____.

Reading

Choose the best answer.

1. ( ) What does the GPS do?
   A: It tells people their exact location.
   B: It flies airplanes and drives cars.
   C: It shows people how to fly 20,000 kilometers above the Earth.
   D: It solves everybody's troubles.

2. ( ) To use the GPS, a person needs _____.
   A: a satellite   B: a car or airplane
   C: a system of things in space   D: a special device

3. ( ) What does "go from A to B" mean?
   A: say one thing and then another
   B: move from one place to another
   C: spell something well
   D: learn to do something

4. ( ) Which of the following is true?
   A: The GPS satellites are on the Earth.
   B: The GPS cannot help people in the mountains.
   C: A person doesn't need to be on the ground to use the GPS.
   D: There are very few uses for the GPS.

Grammar

Put the words in the correct order.

1. in dangerous It's bad drive weather to

   _____.

2. easier GPS flying makes The

   _____.

3. was The couldn't hiker out figure he where

   _____.

Answer Key

Unit 1

Vocabulary
1. changes
2. world
3. alone
4. traditional

Reading
1. D   2. D
3. B   4. C

Grammar
1. played
2. sent
3. changed
4. was

Unit 2

Vocabulary
1. mood
2. advice
3. hobby
4. personality

Reading
1. C   2. B
3. A   4. B

Grammar
1. We usually go swimming on Saturday
2. She is sometimes very funny.
   She is very funny sometimes.
3. Is she always ready to listen?

Unit 3

Vocabulary
1. traffic
2. river
3. Visitors
4. sights

Reading
1. C   2. C
3. A   4. D

Grammar
1. Can't we wait here?
2. Can we get a taxi here?
3. We can't get off here.

Unit 4

Vocabulary
1. forecast
2. cloudy
3. currently
4. partly

Reading
1. D   2. C
3. B   4. B

Grammar
1. Will it be sunny in Boston today?
   Will it be sunny today in Boston?
2. Is it going to be partly cloudy?
3. It might be partly sunny tomorrow.

Answers

Unit 5

Vocabulary
1. vacation
2. natural
3. travel
4. cross

Reading
1. B   2. A
3. D   4. B

Grammar
1. It's a good way to travel and a great vacation.
   It's a good way to travel, and it's a great vacation.
2. You can see the mountains and the lakes.
3. It passes by Lake Ontario and Niagara Falls

Unit 6

Vocabulary
1. delicious
2. Certainly
3. terrible
4. customer

Reading
1. D   2. D
3. B   4. B

Grammar
1. C   2. D
3. B   4. A

Unit 7

Vocabulary
1. speed
2. match
3. extremely
4. strong

Reading
1. D   2. A
3. C   4. A

Grammare
1. C   2. A
3. D   4. B

Unit 8

Vocabulary
1. memories
2. final
3. attend
4. university

Reading
1. A   2. D
3. A   4. C

Grammar
1. We took a lot of pictures.
2. They had a great time together.
3. All of them were a little sad.
4. Did they attend the same university?

Unit 9

Vocabulary
1. wonderful   2. truth
3. Check   4. reply

Reading
1. B   2. C
3. C   4. A

Grammar
1. I didn't check my email.
2. You didn't ask about my work.
3. You didn't attach the photo.
4. She didn't tell me about her plans.

Answers

Unit 10

Vocabulary
1. comfortable
2. stone
3. protect
4. enemy

Reading
1. B   2. D
3. D   4. A

Grammar
1. C   2. D
3. A   4. B

Unit 11

Vocabulary
1. imagine
2. opinion
3. cash
4. responsible

Reading
1. C   2. D
3. C   4. C

Grammar
1. thinks
2. don't
3. think
4. doesn't

Unit 12

Vocabulary
1. signature
2. total
3. business
4. receipt

Reading
1. A   2. C
3. A   4. B

Grammar
1. business, busy
2. expire
3. sign, receipt
4. type

Unit 13

Vocabulary
1. jokes
2. arrive
3. probably
4. package

Reading
1. D   2. B
3. D   4. C

Grammar
1. I really had a great day.
   I had a really great day.
2. Mr. Lane told me I passed the exam.
3. I laughed at his jokes a lot.
   I laughed a lot at his jokes.

Answers

Unit 14

Vocabulary
1. shape
2. hang
3. rainbow
4. Make sure

Reading
1. D
2. C
3. C
4. A

Grammar
1. D
2. C
3. B
4. A

Unit 15

Vocabulary
1. fair
2. members
3. disagree
4. complain

Reading
1. C
2. B
3. B
4. D

Grammar
1. B
2. D
3. A
4. C

Unit 16

Vocabulary
1. peaceful
2. kilometers
3. capital
4. temple

Reading
1. D
2. D
3. B
4. A

Grammar
1. Shanghai is an interesting city on the east coast of China.
2. Singapore is a small, modern country in Southeast Asia.
3. Kyoto is a beautiful city on the island of Honshu.

Unit 17

Vocabulary
1. music
2. total
3. sales
4. pop

Reading
1. A
2. C
3. C
4. B

Grammar
1. price
2. percent
3. sold
4. sales

Unit 18

Vocabulary
1. emotion
2. heavy
3. wild
4. species

Reading
1. C
2. D
3. B
4. A

Grammar
1. In some countries they work.
2. They live for a long time.
3. We are protecting them from hunters.
4. People kill them for their tusks.

Unit 19

Vocabulary
1. relax
2. casual
3. pressure
4. snacks

Reading
1. D
2. A
3. D
4. B

Grammar
met, brought, laughed, lasted

Answers

Unit 20

Vocabulary
1. include
2. popular
3. order
4. set up

Reading
1. D 2. C
3. B 4. A

Grammar
1. This game is easy to learn.
2. It is always nice to win.
3. I think it is fun to play.
4. It is necessary to hit the 9 ball last.

Unit 21

Vocabulary
1. attention
2. grow
3. flower
4. daily

Reading
1. B 2. C
3. A 4. C

Grammar
1. a lot of
2. much
3. a few
4. a lot of

Unit 22

Vocabulary
1. stomach
2. spicy
3. medicine
4. careful

Reading
1. D 2. D
3. B 4. A

Grammar
1. B 2. D
3. A 4. C

Unit 23

Vocabulary
1. remember
2. link
3. add
4. updates

Reading
1. C 2. C
3. D 4. A

Grammar
1. The Earth is like a big blue marble.
2. Please sign my personal guestbook.
3. My website has many different parts.
4. Do you know another cool website?

Unit 24

Vocabulary
1. area
2. formally
3. suit
4. gentleman

Reading
1. D 2. A
3. D 4. B

Grammar
1. I used to work at night.
2. They used to be businessmen.
3. I'm not used to cold weather.

Unit 25

Vocabulary
1. view
2. respect
3. poem
4. experience

Reading
1. C 2. D
3. B 4. D

Grammar
1. C 2. A
3. D 4. B

Answers

Unit 26

Vocabulary
1. conversation
2. pet
3. dream
4. perfect

Reading
1. C 2. D
3. D 4. D

Grammar
1. It's a new magazine with a lot of articles about fashion.
2. It's a monthly magazine for young people.
3. Here's a beautiful photograph from a fashion magazine.

Unit 27

Vocabulary
1. decision 2. behave
3. aware   4. affect

Reading
1. C 2. B
3. D 4. B

Grammar
form, hard, carefully, change, fast

Unit 28

Vocabulary
1. cheat
2. excellent
3. price
4. honest

Reading
1. C 2. C
3. B 4. D

Grammar
1. C 2. A
3. D 4. B

Unit 29

Vocabulary
1. B 2. D
3. A 4. B

Reading
1. C 2. C
3. C 4. A

Grammar
1. taught
2. bought
3. thought
4. caught

Unit 30

Vocabulary
1. wood
2. interesting
3. Tie
4. carry

Reading
1. D 2. C
3. D 4. B

Grammar
1. is used   2. are used
3. uses   4. used

Answers

Unit 31

Vocabulary
1. dangerous
2. catch
3. appreciate
4. weekend

Reading
1. D 2. D
3. B 4. C

Grammar
1. catch   2. arrive
3. work   4. put out

Unit 32

Vocabulary
1. vegetable
2. chop
3. Enjoy
4. ingredients

Reading
1. B 2. C
3. B 4. C

Grammar
1. Cut the lettuce into small pieces.
2. Don't use too much mustard.
3. What kind of sauce do you like?

Unit 33

Vocabulary
1. lessons
2. taste
3. guide
4. concert

Reading
1. B 2. D
3. C 4. B

Grammar
1. every   2. Each
3. per   4. all

Unit 34

Vocabulary
1. rich   2. ancient
3. trade   4. thick

Reading
1. C 2. A
3. A 4. D

Grammar
1. D 2. C
3. A 4. B

Unit 35

Vocabulary
1. together
2. understand
3. huge
4. secret

Reading
1. B 2. C
3. B 4. A

Grammar
1. What should I do?
2. Should I tell her?
3. Should we keep it a secret?
4. I think we should tell her.

Unit 36

Vocabulary
1. forget
2. Blow
3. empty
4. gently

Reading
1. C 2. A
3. B 4. D

Grammar
1. quietly   2. calm
3. gently   4. fresh

Answers

Unit 37

Vocabulary
1. material
2. famous
3. quality
4. machine

Reading
1. B   2. C
3. D   4. A

Grammar
1. She has some beautiful rugs from this village.
2. These rugs are handmade in small villages.
3. I want to buy the silk rug in that shop.

Unit 38

Vocabulary
1. obey
2. accidents
3. causing
4. patient

Reading
1. C   2. A
3. B   4. A

Grammar
1. The accident was caused by speeding.
2. Many people are killed each year.
3. Five people were hurt in the accident.
4. The number of accidents was reduced.

Unit 39

Vocabulary
1. expression
2. communicate
3. deaf
4. meaning

Reading
1. D   2. B
3. A   4. B

Grammar
1. They talk with their hands.
2. It's a language with a grammar.
3. Point at your head with your finger.
4. Can deaf people communicate with non-deaf people?

Unit 40

Vocabulary
1. weather
2. location
3. exactly
4. solve

Reading
1. A   2. D
3. B   4. C

Grammar
1. It's dangerous to drive in bad weather.
2. The GPS makes flying easier.
3. The hiker couldn't figure out where he was.

For the Teacher • Read 100

Series Format

This book is the third in a series of four readers called The Read and Learn Series for beginning-level students. There are 40 units in each book. The readings in this book average about 100 words in length, and a total of just over 800 different words are used in the 40 readings. A summary of the series is below:

Book One: Read 50
50-Word Reading Passages
at the 600-word level

Book Two: Read 75
75-Word Reading Passages
at the 700-word level

Book Three: Read 100
100-Word Reading Passages
at the 800-word level

Book Four: Read 125
125-Word Reading Passages
at the 900-word level

The simple and easy-to-use units follow the same two-page format in all four volumes. A reading is followed by three short exercises that correlate with and expand upon the topical and linguistic content in the reading. Answers to the exercises are found at the back of the book.

The content of the units is broad and comprehensive in its appeal and may be used by learners from middle school to community college, and even beyond.

Reading Passages

The readings in the books include a variety of written material: articles, stories, conversations, menus, charts, diagrams, schedules, and Internet pages and messages. The readings are intended to be entertaining, informative, and useful. They focus on the various reading skills required for living and learning in our contemporary English-speaking world. They are international in scope to stimulate interest in and knowledge of other places and cultures, from the Amazon to Mount Fuji, and to emphasize that English is an international language.

Exercises

Following each reading there are **three types of exercises.** The first is a simple multiple choice exercise that focuses on the meaning and use of selected **vocabulary** items from the reading. In general, the items are used in a context that is somewhat different from the context in the reading. The **reading** exercise checks the students' comprehension of the reading. It requires the students to find specific information and to infer additional, more implicit meanings in the text. The **grammar** exercise expands on a grammatical point (ex: pronoun forms, verb tenses, plurality) or grammatical structure (ex: word order, subject-verb agreement) encountered in the reading. All three exercises require the students to examine the details of the reading passage.

Using the Books

The format of the four-book series is simple and easy to use, allowing for its use by individuals working in an independent mode or by students in a teacher-guided formal class.

Independent Study Mode.

The answers in the back of the book allow learners to work on their language skills completely independently or to use the material as a supplement to a formal study program. The 160 units in the complete series give self-studying learners sufficient material for several hours of study. The progression of the units from short to longer passages provides controlled challenge and comprehensible input. As the passages increase in length and in vocabulary level, the learners' "known" language also increases to meet the challenge of dealing with the "unknowns" of the passages. The uniformity of the units allows the learners the opportunity to focus on the language and not waste time trying to figure out what to do from unit to unit. Most important, perhaps, by following through the entire series, the learners will experience the satisfaction of feeling and recognizing progress.

Formal Class Mode.

Using the books as part of ongoing class work can be done in a variety of ways. A simple and effective procedure is outlined below:

1) Pre-reading preparation. Introduce the nature of the topic and engage the students in a discussion or question-answer session that activates what they may already know about the topic.

2) Initial, silent reading. The students read the passage silently with (or without, as you prefer) their dictionaries to gain an overall understanding. Depending on the level of the class, one to three minutes should be sufficient for this.

3) Reading aloud. This can be done by the teacher, or by students taking turns. A pause for questions and clarification can be added after each sentence or only after the entire passage.

4) Doing the exercises. This can be done individually, but it is often more effective to pair the students and have them work cooperatively. Simply put, two heads are better than one, and the practice of working and learning together can be a very valuable learning experience in itself.

5) Checking the answers. Self-checking or paired checking may generate some questions which should be clarified either as a whole-class activity or as the teacher circulates and responds to individuals or pairs.

6) Discussion. A teacher-led or small group discussion of the content gives the students the opportunity to use the language they already command to talk about new information with newly acquired knowledge and skill (new words, phrases, structures).

7) Writing. The students can keep a notebook or journal and record a sentence or two ("Today, I learned . ."), or perhaps a paragraph stimulated by the reading. An alternative is to do a short dictation using sentences based on the information in the reading.

Semi-Independent Study.

The material can be used in a formal program by having the students read the material and do the exercises out of class. For example, a unit is assigned for homework, and is followed by a brief review the next day. An alternative is a teacher-made quiz to keep the students on task.

Using the CD

A CD is available for each book. It is an optional element, but its use may provide an important and valuable extra dimension to the reading program. Obviously, the CD offers an opportunity for the students to hear a standard pronunciation and phrasing of the text. This can be a very important supplement to an independent study mode, and it may also be very useful in a setting where the teacher's own pronunciation is too heavily influenced by their native language. The CD can also be used to work on listening comprehension. It can be played in class before or after the reading, and the students can follow along by looking at the reading as they listen.

Other materials from Pro Lingua

Legends: 52 People Who Made a Difference
Graded readings from American history – beginner to intermediate. There are 13 units, each with four readings of 100, 150, 200, and 250 words. The legendary people covered in the units are folk heroes, Civil War and anti-slavery heroes, Native Americans, inventors and scientists, educators and reformers, adventurers, human rights leaders, business and labor leaders, famous presidents, military leaders and heroes, writers, entertainers, and sports heroes. Personal and historical time lines are designed for controlled practice of language structures and to stimulate conversation about American culture and history. CD available.

American Holidays: Exploring Traditions, Customs, & Backgrounds
An intermediate reader explaining each of the official national holidays, three cultural holidays (Chinese New Year, Kwanzaa, and Cinco de Mayo), and Christian, Muslim, and Jewish religious holidays. Exercises practice vocabulary building skills, discussion, and Web research. CD available.

Surveys for Conversation
48 surveys designed for beginning to intermediate students – before class they read the surveys and fill them out with their personal information and opinions. In class they enjoy lively conversations which everyone is prepared to participate in. Topics include family, friendship, pets, shopping, clothes, TV, music, computers, space, celebrations, love, marriage, birth & death, work, books, health, summer, winter, crime, war & peace, AD 2100, and the environment.

Do As I Say: Operations, Procedures, and Rituals
A TPR classic revised and updated. Fun activities are ideal for building vocabulary, confidence with grammar, and accuracy in giving and taking instructions.

The Sanchez Family: Now, Tomorrow, and Yesterday
A first book for beginning ESl/EFL students which in a few pages teaches three survival tenses: present progressive, going-to future, and past.

English Interplay
Beginning to intermediate texts for basic English, focused primarily on interactive activities in the classroom using many different approaches and techniques to build vocabulary and all language skills.

To order or for information on these and other materials, contact
www.ProLinguaAssociates.com or 800-366-4775